Table of Contents

FOREWORD

THERE'S REDNECKS & ROUGHNECKS & HOLLOR FOLK

   & YUPPIES

BIG DOGS AND FAT DOGS AND OLD DOGS AND PUPPIES

THERE'S RUSSIAN FOOD, POLISH FOOD, ITALIAN AND FRENCH

COOKIN REDNECK ROAD KILL IS REALLY A CINCH

IT'S GOT REAL GOOD RECIPES, THE BEST I EVER SAW

SOME ARE REAL EASY, YOU JUST EAT THE MEAT RAW

REDNECKS ARE DIFFERENT, BUT THEY *ARE* PEOPLE TOO

THEY MIND THEIR OWN BUSINESS & DON'T CARE WHAT

    YOU DO

BUT ALL REDNECKS AGREE AND THEY STRONGLY SUGGEST

THAT THEIR WAY OF COOKIN IS BY FAR THE BEST

SO I TALKED TO SOME PEOPLE AND MADE UP THIS BOOK

THEY SAID THIS IS THE WAY THAT ALL REDNECKS COOK

WHEN THEY ASKED ME FOR SUPPER, I GOT WHITE AS A SHEET

CAUSE THEY SERVED THE SAME FOOD THAT THEIR DOGS

   WOULDN'T EAT

WHEN YOU LOOK AT THIS BOOK, YOU WILL KNOW IT'S

   NOT TRUE

NOBODY COULD EAT WHAT THIS BOOK SAYS THEY DO

IT'S REALLY ALL FICTION, BUT PLEASE TAKE A LOOK

I JUST WROTE IT ALL DOWN AND MADE IT A BOOK.

THE REAL REDNECK

HIS FIRST TEN YEARS WERE SPENT UNDERNEATH A CAR

AND THE NEXT TWENTY-FIVE IN THE BEER JOINTS AND BARS

HE RAISES PLOT DOGS AND LIVES BACK IN THE HILLS

HE DRINKS HOMEMADE LIQUOR AND EATS DEAD ROADKILLS

HE CAN BE FROM UP A HOLLER IN WV

THE SWAMPS OF LOUISIANA OR THE HILLS OF TENNESSEE

HE THROWS BEER CANS OUT OF HIS JACKED UP TRUCK

AND MAKES HIS OLD LADY PUSH WHEN HIS TRUCK GETS STUCK

HE'S GOT TATTOOS ON HIS HAIRY CHEST AND SCARS ACROSS
   HIS FACE

HE CAN'T SIT DOWN AND HAVE ONE BEER — HE HAS TO HAVE
   A CASE

HE BEATS HIS WIFE — WON'T TAKE A BATH AND DRINKS
   WHISKEY WITH HIS PIZZA

WHEN YOU EXTEND YOUR ARM TO SHAKE HIS HAND HE
   BURPS AND SAYS, "GLAD TA MEETCHA"

POSSUM ON THE HALF SHELL

DEEP IN THE SOUTH IS WHERE IT ALL BEGAN

WHERE FUZZY LITTLE CRITTERS CALLED POSSUMS RAN

THEY'RE DUMBER THAN NAILS AND THEY'RE SLOW ON
THEIR FEET

THEY'VE BEEN RUN DOWN FOR YEARS ON THE ROADS AND
THE STREETS

THEIR BACKS GOT TOUGH BY BEIN SCRAPED UP BY CARS

AND OVER THE YEARS THEY GOT REAL BAD SCARS

THEY'VE BEEN CHEWED ON AND KICKED AND BEAT ALL
TO HELL

AND THROUGH EVOLUTION THEY DEVELOPED A SHELL

COOK AN ARMADILLO BURGER WITH SOME COLE SLAW
AND FRIES

MAKE AN ARMADILLO STEW OR AN ARMADILLO PIE

USE YOUR RECIPE FOR POSSUM — IT'LL DO JUST AS WELL

THE ONLY DIFFERENCE IN THE TWO IS ONE HAS A SHELL

IF YA COOK IT ALL DAY YA WON'T COOK IT ENOUGH

'CAUSE SOMETHIN THAT DUM HAS GOT TO BE TOUGH.

HOOVER HOGS

I MET A MAN FROM ALABAM IN A BEER JOINT IN THE SOUTH

HE WAS DRINKIN BEER AND TELLIN JOKES WITH OYSTERS IN
HIS MOUTH

HE HAD A 4-WHEEL DRIVE WITH A RIFLE RACK
AND THE BACK WAS FULL OF DOGS

HE'D BEEN OUT HUNTIN HALF THE NIGHT AND HE'D CAUGHT
SOME HOOVER HOGS

WHAT THE HECK'S A HOOVER HOG? I SAT THERE AND I
THOUGHT

WHAT KIND OF CREATURE WAS IT THAT HIS HOOVER HOG
DOGS HAD CAUGHT?

HE SAID BACK IN THE THIRTIES WHEN HOOVER WAS OUR CHIEF

WE STARTED COOKING HOOVER HOGS — THAT'S ALL THERE
WAS TO EAT

WALK OUTSIDE AND TAKE A LOOK, BUT WATCH OUT FOR MY
DOGS

AND IN A BAG WERE SEVERAL OF WHAT HE CALLED HOOVER
HOGS

SOMETIMES ITS HARD TO GET THESE CRAZY RECIPES TO
RHYME

BUT ALL HE HAD WAS POSSUMS — HELL WE EAT THEM *ALL*
THE TIME.

ROCKY MOUNTAIN ROAD KILL OYSTERS

CUT SOME OYSTERS FROM A BEEF OR A BIG BULL MOOSE

OR A WHITE TAIL BUCK OR A LONGNECK GOOSE

ANY MALE ROAD KILL WOULD DO JUST FINE

GET YOUR OYSTERS WHERE YOU WANT, JUST DON'T BOTHER
    MINE

THEY'RE PACKED TWO IN A BAG AND THE MEATS REAL SWEET

ROCKY MOUNTAIN OYSTERS ARE REAL GOOD TO EAT

TAKE EM HOME AND SLICE EM AND ROLL EM IN SOME FLOUR

ADD SOME GARLIC SALT AND PEPPER AND FRY EM FOR AN
    HOUR

THE ONLY WAY TO SERVE EM IS HOT FROM THE GREASE

YOU SHOULD GIVE YOUR WIFE SOME AND YOUR KIDS A LITTLE
    PIECE

TO GIVE YOUR WIFE SOME WOULD BE A WISE CHOICE

OR YOU COULD WAKE UP WITH A HIGH PITCHED VOICE.

MOOSE LIPS

ROAD KILL MOOSE WITH HIS ANTLERS IN THE TREES

HIS HAIR WAS KNOCKED OFF AND NOW IT'S BLOWIN IN THE
BREEZE

TO HIT A MOOSE WITH ANY TRUCK COULD TRULY BE A BITCH

HIS LIPS WERE LAYING IN THE ROAD AND MY FENDER IN THE
DITCH

PICK THE LIPS UP OFF THE ROAD AND PUT THEM IN YOUR
TRUCK

BE CAREFUL WHERE YA PUT YOUR LIPS, THEY JUST MIGHT
PUCKER UP

LIPS ARE GOOD WITH EGGS AND TOAST REAL EARLY IN THE
MORN

OR SOAK EM IN SOME SOY SAUCE AND SERVE EM WITH SOME
CORN

MAKE SOME MOOSE LIP HOTDOGS OR MAKE SOME MOOSE LIP
STEW

AND THE HIGHEST FASHION YOU CAN FIND ARE FANCY
MOOSE LIP SHOES

ROADKILL SQUIRREL SQUARES

FIND SOME FLATTENED SQUIRREL MEAT AND PICK OUT ALL

    THE HAIRS

TAKE IT TO THE KITCHEN AND CUT IT INTO SQUARES

MARINATE IT OVERNIGHT IN A BOWL OF BOOZE

THEN SLICE SOME REAL FRESH VEGETABLES — ANY KIND YOU

    CHOOSE

MIX YOUR VEGGIES AND YOUR SQUIRREL AND FRY EM IN A

    SKILLET

THEN TAKE THE BOOZE LEFT IN YOUR BOWL AND TIP IT UP

    AND KILL IT

COOK YOUR VEGGIES AND YOUR SQUIRREL UNTIL THEY SMELL

    REAL NICE

SERVE EM WITH SOME MUSTARD GREENS UPON A BED OF

    RICE.

FOX BALLS

FIND AN ARCTIC, A GREY, OR A BIG RED FOX

SCRAPE IT OFF THE ROAD AND PUT IT IN A BOX

TAKE IT HOME TO YOUR PRESSURE COOKER AND THROW IT
   RIGHT IN

LET IT COOK A HALF HOUR THEN PULL OFF THE SKIN

PUT WHAT'S LEFT OF THE FOX BACK INTO THE POT

PUT THE LID BACK ON AND COOK IT A LOT

RUN HIM THROUGH A MEAT GRINDER BONES AND ALL

THEN ROLL IT ALL UP INTO LITTLE BITTY BALLS

YOU CAN FRY EM OR BAKE EM OR JUST EAT EM RAW

BUY YOURSELF A CASE OF BEER AND HAVE YOURSELF A BALL.

ROAD TOAD — ALA MODE

TAKE A BUCKET FULL OF TOADS FROM A NEARBY STREET

GREEN TOADS ARE BETTER, CAUSE THEY HAVE BETTER MEAT

MAKE UP A PIE SHELL OR BUY IT AT THE STORE

YOU CAN MAKE YOURSELF ONE OR EVEN THREE OR FOUR

LET EM COOK IN THE OVEN AND SIT BACK AND DROOL

PUT EM ON THE WINDOW SILL AND LET THE PIES COOL

ADD SOME HOMEMADE ICE CREAM — VANILLA OR PEACH

TOAD PIE GROWS ON YA LIKE A BLOOD SUCKIN LEECH.

ROADKILL STEW

GRAB A POKE AND LEAVE THE HOUSE BEFORE THE MORNIN'
    DEW

AND TELL YOUR MAW YOU'RE GOIN TO FIND SOME MEAT FOR
    ROADKILL STEW

GET ANYTHING YA FIND THAT'S DEAD, MOST ANYTHING WILL
    DO

A POSSUM, SKUNK OR DEAD GROUNDHOG OR ONE REAL FAT
    RACCOON

TAKE EM HOME AND SKIN EM OUT AND CHOP THE MEAT
    REAL FINE

CUT SOME TATERS AND SOME CARROTS UP AND POUR A
    GLASS OF WINE

ADD SOME ONIONS AND SOME GARLIC AND SALT THE STEW
    TO TASTE

TO LEAVE A VARMENT ON THE ROAD WOULD BE AN AWFUL
    WASTE

BOIL IT HARD FOR QUITE A WHILE AND WHEN THE STEW
    GETS DONE

BE SURE TO PUT SOME HOT SAUCE IN AND SERVE WITH
    HOMEMADE BUNS.

STATE BIRD (UNDER GLASS)

A WREN OR A ROBIN OR A BOB WHITE QUAIL

IF YA KILL STATE BIRDS, YOU'RE GONNA GO TO JAIL

YA GOTTA FIND EM DEAD ON THE ROAD OR THE STREET

THEY CALL EM STATE BIRDS CAUSE THEY HAVE THE
    BEST MEAT

LAY THEM ON YOUR DASHBOARD IN MID-JULY

JUST ROLL UP YOUR WINDOWS AND LET YOUR BIRDS FRY

TURN ON THE DEFROST AND LET YOUR MOTOR RUN

WAIT A LITTLE WHILE AND THE BIRDS WILL BE DONE

SO TRY SOMETHIN NEW — IT'S EASY AND ITS FAST

AND SERVE A SPECIAL FRIEND STATE BIRD UNDER GLASS.

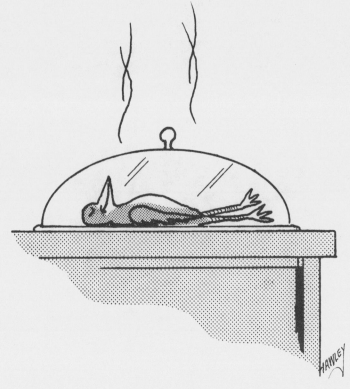

GUESS THAT MESS

GATHER UP SOME ROAD KILL THAT'S LAID AROUND FOR

    YEARS

INVITE SOME BUDDIES OVER AND DRINK A BUNCH OF BEERS

USE ANY KIND OF CRITTERS, CAUSE IT REALLY DOESN'T

    MATTER

JUST THINKIN ABOUT CHOWIN DOWN CAN MAKE A FELLER

    FATTER

MIX IT ALL TOGETHER IN A GREAT BIG BOWL

GUESS THAT MESS IS GOOD FOR YOUR SOUL

ADD GARLIC AND ONIONS AND A TOUCH OF WHITE PEPPER

HOLLER AT YOUR FRIENDS TO GET READY FOR SUPPER

DUMP IT IN A TURKEY COOKER — ALL THAT YOU CAN GET

THE FIRST TIME I MADE IT MY MAMA HAD A FIT

YOUR FRIENDS WILL ALL LOVE IT — YOU'LL BE QUITE A

    SUCCESS

WHEN YOU GIVE EM TWENTY DOLLARS IF THEY GUESS THAT

    MESS.

12

ALLIGATOR TAIL

TAKE A ROADKILL GATOR TAIL FROM DOWN IN MISSISSIP

AND START SOME RED HOT COALS IN YOUR BAR-B-Q PIT

SKIN OUT YOUR TAIL — THERE'S NO HAIR OR FEATHERS

THEN WRAP IT IN SOME FOIL WITH SOME HALAPENA PEPPERS

NOT TOO MANY PEPPERS, CAUSE THEY DO GIVE QUITE A ZIP

THE FIRST PIECE I EVER HAD WAS SO HOT I ALMOST FLIPPED

COOK YOUR TAIL FOR QUITE A WHILE BUT CHECK IT NOW
AND THEN

TO LET A ROADKILL GATER BURN WOULD BE AN AWFUL SIN

TAKE IT OUT AND SLICE IT UP AND COOK SOME BEANS AND
KALE

AND FETCH YA SOMETHIN GOOD TO DRINK AND ENJOY A
PIECE OF TAIL

WHEN YOU EAT YOUR TAIL, TAKE YOUR TIME AND NEVER EAT
TOO FAST

CAUSE A PIECE OF TAIL IS HARD TO FIND AND IT JUST MIGHT
BE YOUR LAST

SO GO OUT EARLY ON THE BEACH, BEFORE THE BOATS SET
SAIL

WHO KNOWS, YOU MIGHT GET LUCKY AND PICK UP A PIECE
OF TAIL.

BRYAN'S ASS

I'VE GOT A COUSIN IN THE COUNTRY WHO RAISES CATTLE AND
   HOGS

A BUNCH OF WOOLY SHEEP AND SOME SHEEP HERDIN' DOGS

BRYAN WORKS HARD FOR SIX STRAIGHT DAYS

PICKIN CORN, PLOWIN FIELDS, SHEARIN' SHEEP AND BAILIN'
   HAY

A HERD OF DONKEYS CROSSED HIS FARM AND BEFORE THEY
   ALL GOT PAST

HE ROPED A DONKEY FOR HIMSELF AND WE CALLED IT
   BRYAN'S ASS

HIS DONKEY WAS A FAITHFUL FRIEND AND FOLLOWED HIM
   EVERYWHERE

ON SUNDAYS HE WOULD RIDE TO TOWN AND WATCH THE
   PEOPLE STARE

HE MADE A SADDLE OUT OF LEATHER, WITH A HORN OF SOLID
   BRASS

THEN EVERYBODY BRYAN KNEW WAS RIDIN BRYAN'S ASS

BRYAN HAD A PEACEFUL LIFE AND STAYED RIGHT ON THE
   FARM

BUT HE WONDERED HOW HIS LIFE WOULD BE WITH A LADY IN
   HIS ARMS

(Cont.)

BRYAN WAS A LONELY MAN, BUT THERE CAME A SWEET
 YOUNG LASS
SHE WOULDN'T KISS HIS HAIRY FACE, BUT SHE WOULD KISS
 BRYAN'S ASS
AND THEN ONE YEAR A FAMINE CAME AND ALL HIS
 LIVESTOCK DIED
AND BRYAN AND HIS BRAND NEW WIFE JUST LAYED AROUND
 AND CRIED
THINGS WOULD GET BETTER THOUGH, CAUSE ALL BAD LUCK
 DOES PASS
BUT THERE'LL BE NO NEED FOR TRACTOR SEATS, 'CAUSE
 BRYAN LOST HIS ASS.

HARDCORE AND HUNGRY

HARDCORE AND HUNGRY AND MORE THAN HALF WAY DRUNK

YOU SHOULD HAVE GONE TO SCHOOL MY FRIEND, NOW
　　YOU'RE JUST A PUNK

HIS HAIR IS LONG AND GREASY AND HIS TEETH ARE ROTTED
　　OUT

HE'LL NEVER REALLY UNDERSTAND WHAT LIFE IS ALL ABOUT

HE WANDERS UP AND DOWN THE ROAD RUNNING FROM THE
　　LAW

UGLY, GRUESOME, STINKIN SCUM, THE WORST I EVER SAW

THE KIND OF GUY WHO STANDS AROUND AND TRIES TO BUM
　　A DIME

THEN GOES UP TO THE CORNER STORE TO BUY A JUG OF WINE

HE EATS BLOODY SICKENING ROTTED FLESH WITHOUT A
　　TOOTH AT ALL

HE GETS DOWN ON HIS HANDS AND KNEES AND SUCKS IT
　　THROUGH A STRAW

WHEN HE'S DONE HE RAISES UP AND PUKES IT ON THE STREET

AND IF YOU ASK HIM HOW IT WAS, HE'LL SAY ITS HARD TO
　　BEAT.

OLD CROW PIE

GET SOME CROWS OFF THE ROAD OR ANYWHERE YOU CAN

WHEN CROWS GET OLD YOU CAN CATCH EM WITH YOUR
HANDS

THEY'RE OLD AND THEY'RE TOUGH AND SOMETIMES THEY
STINK

JUST COOK A CROW PIE AND SEE WHAT YOU THINK

DRIVE TO THE STORE TO BUY SHELLS FOR YOUR PIES

IT WOULD ONLY TAKE A MINUTE AS AN OLD CROW FLIES

THROW YOUR CROWS DOWN ON AN OLD CHOPPIN BLOCK

YA ONLY NEED THREE OR FOUR — YA DON'T NEED A FLOCK

CHOP EM INTO PIECES ABOUT TWO INCHES SQUARE

ADD SOME OLD CROW WHISKEY — AS MUCH AS YOU DARE

DICE TWO RED TOMATOES FRESH OFF THE VINE

A CUP OF CHICKEN WHISKEY AND SOME MUSKYDINE WINE

ADD SOME PURE BROWN SUGAR — ONE BIG CHUNK

IF YA DON'T LIKE THE PIE, YA STILL GET DRUNK

ITS BEST SERVED AFTER A MOOSE LIP STEW

WITH A LITTLE WARM MILK AND A COLD MOUNTAIN DEW.

17

AWESOME POSSUM GRAVY AND BUTTERMILK BISCUITS

AWESOME POSSUM GRAVY AND BUTTERMILK BISCUITS

IT'S HARDER TO SAY IT THAN IT IS TO FIX IT

TAKE A FULL GROWN POSSUM THAT'S WHOLE AND ROUND

WITH A LAST YEARS TOMATO STAKE BEGIN TO POUND

KEEP ON POUNDIN' TIL HE TURNS TO MUSH

STICK A YAM IN HIS MOUTH AND A PICKLE IN HIS TUSH

FLIP HIM AND TURN HIM FROM TIME TO TIME

TIL THE MUSH INSIDE TURNS INTO A SLIME

LET HIM SWELL IN THE SUN TIL FULLY RIPE

THE YAM AND THE PICKLE OTTA FIT REAL TIGHT

IN THE BOTTOM OF THE STOVE THERE'S A NUMBER 8 SKILLET

PULL OUT THE PICKLE AND BEGIN TO FILL IT

SQUEEZE ON THE POSSUM TIL YA GET ALL YA CAN

IF YA GET AN AIR LOCK YOU CAN PULL OUT THE YAM

STIR UNCOVERED OVER MEDIUM HEAT

ADD THE PICKLE AND THE YAM AND SOME STRIPS OF MEAT

CALL YOUR HUSBAND AND THE KIDS AND YOUR NEIGHBOR'S
   SON

YA BETTER CHECK ON THE BISCUITS, CAUSE THE GRAVY'S
   DONE

PORKYPINE

IF YOU HIT A PORKYPINE WAY OUT IN THE STICKS

AND YUR TIRE GOES FLAT 'CAUSE OF PORKYPINE PRICKS

AND YOU LOOK IN THE TRUNK AND YOUR SPARE'S FLAT TOO

WELL, A MANS GOTTA DO WHAT A MANS GOTTA DO

ITS GETTIN DARK OUTSIDE AND YOU'RE HUNGRY AS HELL

AND ITS A FOUR DAY WALK TO THE TACO BELL

SO YA BUILD A BIG FIRE AND WARM UP YOUR FEET

AND TRY YOUR FIRST ROAD KILL PORKYPINE MEAT

TAKE A PAIR OF PLIERS AND PULL OUT THE PRICKS

AND STICK EM BACK IN THE TIRE — THAT WAS EASY TO FIX

HOLD PORKY UP AND RIP OUT HIS GUTS

PUT HIM ON THE FIRE AND WALK BACK TO THE TRUCK

YA GOT YOUR TIRE ALL PLUGGED — NOW YOU JUST NEED
   SOME AIR

DON'T OVERCOOK YOUR PORKYPINE, HE'S BETTER QUITE RARE

(Cont.)

PORKYPINES ARE GOOD, BUT THEY GIVE A FELLER GAS

YA NEED TO THINK OF SOMETHIN QUICK — YA BETTER THINK

    OF SOMETHIN FAST

SAVE UP YOUR GAS FOR THIRTY MINUTES TO AN HOUR

THEN SIT ON YOUR VALVE AND BLOW UP YOUR TIRE

YA FIXED YOUR FLAT TIRE AND DIDN'T EVEN NEED A JACK

MY DADDY ALWAYS TOLD ME — USE YOUR HEAD AND NOT

    YOUR BACK

THIS POEM'S KINDA SICK AND SOME PARTS ARE EVEN GORY

BUT WHAT THE HELL WOULD YOU HAVE DONE IF YOU WERE

    IN THE STORY.

CHIPMONK BISCUITS WITH EGG AND CHEESE

TO MAKE A CHIPMONK BISCUIT WITH EGG AND CHEESE

CUT THE MONK'S LEGS OFF JUST ABOVE THE KNEES

YOU CAN CUT THE HEAD OFF OR LEAVE IT RIGHT ON

BUT A CHIPMONK'S BRAINS ARE THE BEST THING GOIN

HOLD THE MONK IN YOUR HAND AND SQUEEZE HIM REAL
    HARD

HIS GUTS WILL SQUISH OUT — JUST SLING EM IN THE YARD

SPRINKLE WITH SOME FLOUR, THEN FRY EM IN SOME GREASE

PICK A MONK OUT AND TRY A LITTLE PIECE

COOK EM LIKE YOUR BISCUITS — TILL THEY'RE GOLDEN
    BROWN

ADD SOME CHEESE AND A CHICKEN EGG AND SWALLOW EM
    DOWN.

ARMADILLA PIE

ROLL OUT SOME PIE DOUGH AND MOLD IT TO A SHELL

OR BUY YOUR CRUST READY-MADE — WHAT THE HELL

GO FIND AN ARMADILLA IN THE ALABAMA HEAT

AND PUT THE GUTS IN A BAG AND WHAT'S LEFT OF THE MEAT

PICK OFF THE BUGS AND BLOW OFF THE DUST

TAKE EM HOME TO YOUR KITCHEN AND FILL UP YOUR CRUST

ADD SOME HOT SAUCE AND GARLIC AND SOME ONION SLICED

    THIN

MAKE ONE FOR YOURSELF AND COOK ONE FOR A FRIEND

IN AN OVEN COOK YOUR PIE TILL YOUR CRUST IS GOLDEN

    BROWN

AND WHEN THEY'RE DONE YOU'LL KNOW YOU'VE MADE THE

    BEST PIES IN TOWN.

REDNECK HOMEBREW

USE PEACHES, POTATOES, APPLES OR BERRIES

TO MAKE SOME HOMEBREW BEER, WINE OR SHERRY

JUST WASH UP YOUR FRUIT AND PUT IT IN A DRUM

REDNECK HOMEBREW CAN BE A LOT OF FUN

TAKE OFF YOUR BOOTS AND BRUSH OFF YOUR FEET

THROW A BUNCH OF SUGAR IN TO MAKE YOUR BREW SWEET

STOMP ON YOUR FRUIT AND JUMP UP AND DOWN

ADD A BUNCH OF YEAST — NOT MORE THAN A POUND

LET IT SET IN THE CELLAR FOR ALMOST A YEAR

IT TAKES A LONG TIME TO MAKE A REDNECK BEER

BUT THE LONGER YOU LEAVE IT THE STRONGER IT GETS

IT'LL OPEN UP YOUR NOSE AND BURN OFF YOUR LIPS

I'VE DRUNK HOMEBREW BEER SINCE I WAS JUST A KID

I'D OPEN UP A BOTTLE AND THROW AWAY THE LID

THIS BREW IS THE BEST, BUT I DON'T LIKE TO BOAST

TRY A JUG IN THE MORNIN WITH YOUR FRIED EGGS

    AND TOAST.

STEEL BELTED BEAVER BRAINS

STEEL BELTED BEAVER BRAINS, WHAT A SWEET DELIGHT

MOSTLY FLATTENED DURING THE DAY, BUT SOMETIMES LATE
AT NIGHT

STEEL BELTED RADIAL ACROSS THE BEAVER'S FACE

PICK HIS BRAINS UP OFF THE ROAD AND PUT EM ON YOUR
PLATE

TAKE EM HOME AND ROLL EM OUT IN ONE BIG FLATTENED
CAKE

YA CAN FRY EM IN A SKILLET, ALTHOUGH SOME FOLKS LIKE
EM BAKED

WALK OUTSIDE AND BLOW SOME SMOKE OF REEFER THAT
YOU'VE GROWN

YOU'RE FRYING UP THE BEAVER BRAINS, SO WHY NOT FRY
YOUR OWN.

24

CRASHIN' COUNTRY CARIBOU

CRASHIN' COUNTRY CARIBOU — IF YOU HIT ONE ANYPLACE

HE'LL BUST RIGHT THROUGH THE WINDOW GLASS AND HIT

    YOU IN THE FACE

HIS ANTLERS STICKIN THROUGH YOUR CHEST AND POKIN

    THROUGH YOUR SEAT

HIS HOOFS HAVE HIT YOU IN YOUR MOUTH AND BUSTED OUT

    YOUR TEETH

HE FLOPS AND KICKS AND SWINGS AROUND UP FRONT IN

    YOUR CAB

YOU WERE HUNGRY FOR SOME CARIBOU, BUT REALLY NOT

    THIS BAD

SPIT YOUR TEETH OUT IN YOUR HAND AND PUT A BANDAID ON

    YOUR CHEST

AND PULL THE HOGLEG .44 FROM JUST INSIDE YOUR VEST

GO AHEAD AND SHOOT THE THING, IT'S A SHAME YOU HAD TO

    MISS

YOU SHOT YOUR MOTHER IN THE LEG AND KILLED YOUR ONLY

    SIS

ONE GOOD THING HAS COME

    ABOUT FROM THIS AWFUL

    CRASH

YOU'LL NEVER HAVE TO BRUSH

    YOUR TEETH, JUST THROW

    EM IN THE TRASH.

PICKLED POSSUM PARTS

ROADKILL POSSUM PARTS MASHED REAL FLAT

SCRAPED OFF THE ROAD AND THROWN IN A VAT

THERE'S SALT WATER PICKLE BRINE; THE BEST I EVER ATE

YOU CAN EAT IT FROM THE CAN OR EAT IT OFF A PLATE

THERE MAY BE SOME TRACES OF SOME BLACKTOP TAR

OR LITTLE CHUNKS OF METAL FROM UNDERNEATH THE CAR

THERE'S EYEBALLS AND HAIR AND MASHED UP GUTS

EYELIDS AND LIPS AND ALL SORTS OF STUFF

YOU CAN COOK IT LIKE WE DO OR HOWEVER YOU FEEL

BUY A SIX PACK OF BEER AND HAVE A SEVEN COURSE MEAL

ROAD KILL PIZZA PIE

PICK SOME GUTS UP OFF THE ROAD AND GREASE A PIZZA PAN

TOSS THE GUTS UP IN THE AIR AND CATCH EM IN YOUR HAND

MAKE A SAUCE FROM BLOOD AND SLIME AND SMEAR IT ALL
AROUND

ADD SOME PEPPERS GREEN OR RED AND SKUNK MEAT THAT'S
BEEN GROUND

MAKE SOME CHEESE FROM A NANNY GOAT OR JUST A PLAIN
OLE COW

SPREAD IT ON YOUR PIZZA PIE AND COOK IT FOR A WHILE

WHEN ITS DONE, TAKE IT OUT AND SERVE IT ON A PLATE

A REDNECK'S ROADKILL PIZZA PIE IS THE BEST I EVER ATE.

MY EPILEPTIC BEAGLE

WHISKEY JOE, WITH PAPERS TO SHOW, WAS MY FAVORITE
RABBIT DOG

HE HAD FLOPPY EARS AND SAGGY JAWS — THE BEST I EVER
SAW

HE RAN FIELD TRAILS AND WON THE PRIZE A LOT MORE
TIMES THAN NOT

AND SOMETIMES ON HIS BETTER DAYS THE RABBITS WERE
EVEN CAUGHT

HE RAN HIS RABBITS IN A CIRCLE AND HE NEVER TRACKED A
DEER

AND THE STRANGEST THING I EVER SAW HAPPENED JUST LAST
YEAR

I JUMPED A RABBIT AND SURE AS HELL — HE GOT RIGHT ON
HIS TRAIL

THEN HE STOPPED RIGHT IN HIS TRACKS AND STIFFENED UP
HIS TAIL

(Cont.)

HIS LEGS GOT STRAIGHT HE FELL ON HIS HEAD AND

SLOBBERED FROM HIS FACE

WHATEVER IT WAS MY DOGGY HAD, HE REALLY HAD QUITE A

CASE

HE FLOPPED AROUND THERE ON THE GROUND — IT SEEMED

LIKE QUITE A WHILE

I'VE SEEN A LOT OF RABBIT DOGS, BUT NONE WITH WHISKEY'S

STYLE

THEN HE JUMPED UP ON HIS FEET AND SMOOTHED OUT ALL

HIS HAIR

AND FROM THAT DAY ON WHISKEY JOE RAN RABBITS IN A

SQUARE.

CHICKEN WHISKEY

STEAL A RED BANTY ROOSTER STRAIGHT FROM THE BARN

OR TAKE A ROADSIDE KILL — WHO GIVES A DARN

PUT HIM IN A BARREL AND MASH HIM WITH A STICK

KEEP ON MASHIN TILL THE JUICES ARE THICK

PICK OUT THE FEATHERS BUT LEAVE ALL THE GUTS

THROW THE LEGS AND THE SKIN TO YOUR COON DOG PUPS

ADD THREE HUNKS OF SUGAR AND A HANDFUL OF YEAST

LET IT BREW IN THE SUN FOR TWO OR THREE WEEKS

MAKES A GALLON OF WHISKEY 'BOUT NINETY PROOF

CURES ALL KINDS OF AILMENTS EVEN THE CROUP

NOT AS GOOD AS SOME BREW BUT BETTER THAN MOST

GREAT FOR A PARTY OR A FORMAL TOAST

SO MAKE A BIG BATCH AND SIP IT ALL DAY

MAKES THE HOLLER BOYS COCKY AND THE COUNTRY

    GIRLS LAY

ARMADILLA PARTS

THERE'S ARMADILLA PARTS SCRAPED OFF THE STREET

LITTLE BITS OF SHELL AND MASHED UP MEAT

BONES AND TAIL ALL GROUND REAL FINE

WE LET IT SET FOR A MONTH IN A SALT WATER BRINE

IT'S GOT OUR OWN SPECIAL BLEND OF SOUTHERN SPICE

IT'S A LITTLE BIT HOT BUT IT SURE TASTES NICE

YOU CAN USE YOUR ARMADILLA IN A SOUP OR A STEW

OR EAT IT PLAIN FROM THE CAN, WE DON'T CARE

    WHAT'CHA DO

USE IT IN RECIPES THAT CALL FOR GOOD MEAT

ARMADILLA PARTS ARE REAL HARD TO BEAT

Armadilla
Parts

WOLVERINES

I'VE ALWAYS HEARD THAT WOVERINES WERE KILLERS AND
    THEY'RE MEAN

BUT RIDIN DOWN THE ROAD ONE NIGHT BEAT ALL I'D EVER
    SEEN

I WAS RIDIN SHOTGUN IN A TRUCK THAT WAS DRIVEN BY MY
    WIFE

AND DIDN'T KNOW THAT SOON I WOULD BE THREATENED WITH
    MY LIFE

WHAT WE SAW IN THE ROAD WAS WILDER THAN YOUR
    DREAMS

CAUSE UP AHEAD WE SAW A PACK OF RABID WOLVERINES

MY WIFE HAD MENTIONED SHE WOULD LIKE SOME WOLVERINE
    IN HER KETTLE

SO SHE BUCKLED UP HER BELT AND PUT THE PEDAL TO THE
    MEDAL

WE HIT ONE GOOD AND HE LOOKED LIKE HE'D BEEN RUN
    THROUGH A BLENDER

BUT THE BIGGEST ONE WAS HANGIN ON AND CHEWIN ON OUR
    FENDER

(Cont.)

I'D NEVER SEEN A WOLVERINE THAT TRIED TO KILL A TRUCK

HE ATE THE GRILL AND FENDER OFF AND THEN HE LOOKED
AT US

HIS EYES WERE RED AND BULGING AND HIS TEETH WERE
REALLY WHITE

I THOUGHT FOR SURE MY WIFE AND I WERE GOING TO DIE
THAT NIGHT

WHAT HAPPENED NEXT I'LL HAVE TO SAY CAUSE I KNOW
YOU'LL NEVER GUESS

MY WIFE REACHED OUT AND SLAPPED THE THING CAUSE SHE
HAD P.M.S.

SHE BEAT AND KICKED AND BITCHED IT OUT AND PULLED THE
VARMENT'S HAIR

I COULDN'T STAND TO WATCH THE FIGHT, IT WAS MORE THAN
I COULD BEAR

I YELLED TO HER TO SEE IF SHE COULD USE ANY ASSISTANCE

SHE HOLLERED BACK, STAY OUT OF THIS, SHUT UP AND KEEP
YOUR DISTANCE

I DIDN'T KNOW WHO TO BE SORRY FOR, MY WIFE OR THE UGLY
CRITTER

BUT THANKS TO FORDS AND PMS WE HAD WOLVERINE FOR
DINNER

THE GHOST OF NIMROD KANE

NIMROD KANE WAS UGLY AND MEAN AND HE WAS ONLY SEEN
AT NIGHT

HE WALKED THE ROADS WITH RAGGED CLOTHES AND HE
VANISHED BEFORE DAYLIGHT

THEY SAY HE DIED 50 YEARS AGO FROM A SHOTGUN BLAST TO
HIS FACE

BUT WHEN THEY DUG UP NIMROD'S GRAVE ONE NIGHT ALL
THEY FOUND WAS AN EMPTY SPACE

HE EATS CATS AND DOGS AND DEAD GROUNDHOGS AND
ANYTHING DEAD ON THE STREET

HE STUFFS HIS BLOODY AND GRUESOME FACE WITH ROTTEN
AND RANCID MEAT

THE OLD FOLKS SAY IN NIMROD'S YOUTH HE WAS A VERY
PRODUCTIVE LAD

BUT SOMETHING SNAPPED IN NIMROD'S BRAIN AND HE
MURDERED HIS MOM AND DAD

THE SHERIFF SENT A POSSY OUT OF SIXTEEN MOUNTED MEN

BUT THE POSSY SENT FOR NIMROD KANE WAS NEVER SEEN
AGAIN

THE LAST SIGHTING OF THE GHOST WAS THIRTEEN MONTHS
AGO

WHEN A LOCAL GIRL JUST IN HER TEENS WAS BROKE DOWN
ON THE ROAD

(Cont.)

SHE WAS SCARED SO BAD BY WHAT SHE SAW THAT HER EYES
POPPED OUT ON HER CHEEKS

NOW ALL THAT SWEET YOUNG GIRL CAN DO IS STARE DOWN
AT HER FEET

THEN ONE NIGHT WHILE DRINKING BEER, I'D HAD ALMOST A
CASE

I SET OUT TO FIND THAT UGLY GHOST AND I MET HIM FACE TO
FACE

I COULDN'T BELIEVE WHAT I HAD SEEN BUT BEFORE MY CAR
COULD PASS

I WITNESSED THE DEATH OF NIMROD'S GHOST CAUSE A
POSSUM BONE WAS STUCK IN HIS . . .

BUFFALO WINGS

A COUPLE HUNDRED YEARS AGO WHEN BUFFALO COULD FLY

A MAN NAMED WILLIAM CODY SHOT THEM FROM THE SKY

HE SHOT AND SHOT AND SHOT THE THINGS, HE THOUGHT IT
WAS OK

HE ONLY ATE THE BISONS WINGS AND THREW THE REST AWAY

NOW WHEN YA FIND SOME WINGS THEY'RE GONNA BE REALLY
SMALL

IF YA FIND SOME BUFFALO WITH ANY WINGS AT ALL

FIRST YOU NEED TO FIND A FLOCK OF BUFFALO THAT FLY

JUMP 'EM WITH YOUR BISON DOGS AND SHOOT THEM FROM
THE SKY

IT'S ALWAYS BEST TO SHOOT THE ONES THAT HAVE A GREAT
BIG HUMP

THEY'LL FALL FROM SEVERAL HUNDRED FEET AND HIT WITH
QUITE A THUMP

IT'S ALWAYS NICE TO THINK ABOUT THE TASTY MEAT THEY
BRING

IF YA SHOOT A HUNDRED BUFFALO YOU'LL HAVE TWO
HUNDRED WINGS

EVERYBODY LOVED THE WINGS AND ATE ALL THAT THEY
FOUND

AND NOW THAT ALL THEIR WINGS ARE GONE THEY WALK
UPON THE GROUND

SOAK 'EM IN SOME PEPPER SAUCE THEN ROLL 'EM IN SOME
FLOUR

I LIKE 'EM KIND OF CRISPY SO I FRY 'EM FOR AN HOUR

REAL RECIPES

WILD GAME
AND
COUNTRY
RECIPES

Real "Wild Game" Recipes

Wild game includes all wild animals and wild fowl used for food. The same general rules used for cooking domesticated animals also apply to cooking wild animals. The flavor of most wild meat can be enhanced with onions, garlic, herbs and spices. Here is a chance for you to be creative. Just remember that all white meat should be cooked well done and dark meat is best cooked rare. Both should be served steaming hot.

Wild game is very nutritious, with much more lean than fat and, when cooked properly, the taste is superb. If you are not already a wild game lover, I hope the following recipes will make one of you.

VENISON

Venison is as versatile as beef. Ground, it can be used for spaghetti sauce, meat loaf, cabbage rolls, sausage or burgers and if your kill is older, it might be wise to have it *all* ground. Save your younger, more tender kills for steaks, roasts, fondue, soups, stews, etc., but it is a wild meat that you can enjoy many different ways.

VENISON STEAKS are prepared and served like beef steak, cutting them only about three-quarters of an inch thick. Broil them to your liking, but they are really best rare, sprinkled with garlic and salt and pepper.

DEVILED VENISON is a real treat. To prepare, cut thick slices from rare-roasted venison, make slanting incisions and fill them with a mixture of prepared mustard and salad oil. Brush the slices with melted butter and dredge them with flour. Place on a rack over very hot coals on your grill until brown, turn and quickly brown the other side. Serve with a baked potato and a big spinach salad.

VENISON POT PIE

For this pie, use the neck, breast, flank or any other portions that are not suitable for roasting. Cut the meat free from the bone and into one inch squares. Parboil with a bay leaf till the meat begins to be tender, then season well with salt and pepper. You may add onions, mushrooms, celery, carrots or any other vegetable you desire.

While this is cooking, place the bones and trimmings in a stewpan with a pinch of mace, salt and pepper and enough cold water to cover. Simmer until the water is reduced by one half. Strain, cool and remove the fat. Make a thickening of cornstarch and port wine and add to the broth for a medium thick gravy.

Make a crust of 2 cups of flour, ½ pound of butter, the yolks of two eggs, a teaspoon salt and ½ cup water. Divide crust, roll out and place one-half in bottom of a deep dish pie plate. Add your pieces of meat and any vegetables you may have included, then the gravy and cover with the other crust. Puncture the top crust and bake until golden brown. A good salad and dessert is all you need to make this a very satisfying meal.

CREAMED VENISON

This recipe is used with permission of The Country Publishers, Inc. of Middleburg, Virginia from their Game Cookbook.

4-5 pound round steak
  (venison)
4 medium onions
1 cup sour cream
½ teaspoon marjoram, dried
½ tablespoon salt

1 cup flour
¼ pound butter
½ cup beef broth
4-5 tablespoons grated
  parmesan cheese
¼ tablespoon pepper

Sprinkle both sides of the steak with salt, pepper, marjoram, and flour. Then pound the meat with a wooden mallet until the flour disappears. Chop the onions into thick slices. Sauté the onions with the butter in a large, heavy skillet. When onions are honey-colored, remove them from the skillet. Place the steak in the skillet and brown using high heat. Mix beef broth, sour cream, cooked onions, and cheese, and pour over the meat. Simmer slowly until tender, usually about one hour. This is so good that leftovers can be eaten on corn cakes the next morning for breakfast. Serves six.

JEFF'S VENISON MEAT LOAF RECIPE

2½-3 lbs. ground venison
8 ounces Parmesan cheese
6 ounces Italian bread crumbs
3 eggs
1 large onion diced fine

1 green pepper diced fine
2 cloves garlic pressed
Salt and pepper to taste
3 tablespoons brown sugar
½ cup spaghetti sauce (optional)

Combine all ingredients except brown sugar and spaghetti sauce and mix thoroughly in a large mixing bowl. Shape into a loaf and place on an ungreased baking dish. Sprinkle with brown sugar and, if you like, pour just enough spaghetti sauce over the meat loaf to cover it. Bake uncovered in a 350 degree oven for one hour and 15 minutes. Slice and serve with scalloped potatoes and steamed broccoli. The next day, when it is cold, it makes a great sandwich.

To make great Italian meatballs, use the same recipe, but roll the mixture into balls and fry until brown in vegetable oil.

Small Game

BROILED RABBIT

Skin, singe and wipe the rabbit. Prepare for the broiler like chicken and cook over charcoal embers till done. Season with salt and pepper just before it is finished and pour over melted butter, mixed with 2 tablespoons vinegar and a tablespoon of prepared mustard.

WILD RABBIT

This recipe is used with permission of The Country Publishers, Inc. of Middleburg, Virginia from their Game Cookbook.

2 wild rabbits, 1½ pounds each,
   or 1 snowshoe rabbit
1 teaspoon allspice
2 tablespoons butter
½ teaspoon salt
¼ teaspoon celery seed
   or parsley
2 cups chicken stock
1 cup sour cream

½ gallon red wine,
   very inexpensive
1 medium onion, chopped
2 tablespoons lemon juice
½ teaspoon pepper
½ teaspoon ground sage
2 quarts bread crumbs or
   crumbled cornbread
½ cup sherry

Marinate the cleaned rabbits in wine, allspice and chopped onion for two days. Mix stuffing of bread or cornbread crumbs, chicken stock, celery seed, sage, salt, pepper, and finely chopped onion. Pour marinade off the rabbits and rub them with butter and lemon juice. Bake slowly for ½ hour. Take out and stuff. Bake slowly (300°) for another hour. Just before serving pour mixture of sherry and sour cream over the meat. Rabbit is very rich and this recipe will serve eight.

SQUIRREL GRAVY WITH BISCUITS

Skin and clean two medium squirrels. Cut into pieces and put into a pot. Cover with water and cook with a piece of fatback or a couple of strips of bacon until tender. Take squirrel from pot and strip from bones and put back into pot. Make a thickening with ½ cup flour and 1 cup of milk and add to the hot broth. When this thickens, serve over hot, golden brown biscuits or any other meal. Delicious!

ROASTED GROUND HOG

This recipe is used with permission of The Country Publishers, Inc. of Middleburg, Virginia from their Game Cookbook.

2 young ground hogs
2 medium onions, chopped
1 tablespoon pepper
2 cups red wine
1 teaspoon marjoram

4 strips bacon
1 tablespoon salt
¼ pound butter
1 cup chopped celery
1 can of sweet potatoes in syrup

Take two cleaned, skinned ground hogs and soak overnight in salt water. Be certain to remove glands under front and hind legs before soaking. Drain and dry. Wrap each ground hog with two strips of bacon and place in roaster with wine, onions, celery, salt, butter, pepper, and marjoram. Roast at 350 degrees for 1 hour and 15 minutes. Take out and pour can of sweet potatoes and syrup over the meat. Roast 15 more minutes and serve. Young raccoons can be cooked the same way. Serves six.

Fowl

GROUSE

Pluck very carefully, so as not to tear the skin. Draw and wipe, but do not wash. Cut off the head and truss like any other fowl. You may either rub them with butter or fasten thin slices of salt pork all over the breast and thighs. Bake at 300 degrees and baste every few minutes until tender.

Parboil the liver and pound it to a paste. Add butter, salt and cayenne pepper. Serve on toast browned in butter and spread with the liver paste. Delicious with brown gravy.

FILLETS OF GROUSE

If the birds are badly shot to pieces or torn up while dressing, it is often better to fillet and fry them. Season the fillets with salt and pepper and dip them in a mixture of 1 tablespoon of chopped parsley, 1 tablespoon of lemon juice and ½ cup of melted butter. Let this mixture cool on them, then dip in a beaten egg, then in bread crumbs and fry in deep, hot fat for 4 to 6 minutes. Drain and arrange around a mound of your favorite steamed or stir-fried vegetables.

SMOTHERED GROUSE

Pick, singe and sponge as usual. Split in halves as for broiling; rub well with salt and chili powder. Baste with salad oil and brown delicately in a hot skillet. Cover tightly and turn the fire low to allow it to cook in its own steam for a half hour or more. Remove the birds to a platter. Add one cup of brown stock to the pan in which they were browned. Let it simmer enough to make a glaze and pour over the birds. Serve with green peas.

Partridge, pheasant, quail and dove may all be prepared in this same manner.

ROAST WILD TURKEY

This recipe is used with permission of The Country Publishers, Inc. of Middleburg, Virginia from their Game Cookbook.

1 wild turkey, dressed	4 strips bacon
chestnut or cornbread stuffing	1 cup sherry
1 tablespoon pepper	½ tablespoon salt

Turkey has such a soft, mellow flavor that the less you do to disturb it, the better the outcome. To prepare for roasting, wipe turkey clean, inside and out, with a damp cloth. Stuff with a chestnut or bread stuffing, truss, salt and pepper, and place four strips of bacon on breast. Roast uncovered for one hour at 325-350 degrees. After the first hour soak a heavy paper towel with sherry and place over bird. Baste every ten minutes with drippings. Most wild turkeys weigh from eight to fifteen pounds dressed. Roast 15-20 minutes per pound. Be sure to baste frequently. Serves six.

Fish

BAKED FISH

Clean, wipe and dry the fish, rub with salt inside and out, stuff and sew; cut gashes two inches apart on each side so they will alternate and skewer into the shape of an S or an O. Put the fish on a greased baking sheet. Place strips of cotton cloth under the fish, by which it may be lifted from the pan without tearing up the fish. Sprinkle with salt and pepper and place narrow strips of bacon in the gashes. Place in a hot oven (400 degrees) without water. As soon as it begins to brown, baste with hot water and butter every ten minutes. It takes about an hour to cook a four pound fish. Remove to a hot platter. Draw out the string, wipe off all water or fat which remains from the fish and remove the pieces of bacon. Garnish with parsley or water-cress.

STUFFING FOR BAKED FISH

1 cup bread crumbs
1 tablespoon minced onion
2 tablespoons butter
1 egg, beaten with 1 tbsp. water

1 teaspoon chopped parsley
½ teaspoon salt
¼ teaspoon pepper

Mix lightly and stuff fish before baking.

FISH AU GRATIN

3 lbs. fish
2 cups white sauce
½ cup cracker crumbs
2 tablespoons butter
2 tablespoons chopped parsley

½ teaspoon salt
¼ teaspoon pepper
¼ teaspoon cayenne pepper
¼ tsp. celery salt

The fish should be freed from skin and bone and broken into little pieces. Melt the butter and combine with cracker crumbs. Butter a baking dish and place alternate layers of fish and cracker crumbs. Moisten with sauce and sprinkle with seasonings. Sprinkle buttered crumbs over the top and bake in a quick oven for ten or fifteen minutes.

TROUT (Rainbow, Brook, Brown, Cutthroat, Steelhead)

This recipe is used with permission of The Country Publishers, Inc. of Middleburg, Virginia from their Game Cookbook.

6 trout
4 lemons
1 teaspoon pepper
1 teaspoon salt

¼ pound butter
2 ounces white wine
garnish of parsley and
    rosettes of radish

Scale the trout well and cut off heads. Open and clean. Soak at least one hour in cold salted water. Remove from brine and wash. Put on foil or broiler pan. Place one tablespoon of butter inside each fish and then dust with black pepper. Squeeze a liberal amount of lemon juice on each fish, about two tablespoons. Cook for five minutes on each side under hot broiler. Be sure to baste. After it's well saturated with lemon juice and butter, pour the wine over the fish. Serves six.

FISH CROQUETTES

2 cups cold boiled fish
2 cups hot mashed potatoes
1 tablespoon butter
½ cup hot milk

1 egg
1 teaspoon salt
½ teaspoon pepper
1 teaspoon chopped parsley

Pick the fish over carefully to remove skin and bone; mince fine; combine all ingredients, mix thoroughly and let cool. When cold, form into balls, dip into beaten egg, roll in bread crumbs, fry in hot fat. Drain on paper towels.

You can use canned salmon in this recipe, but you will need to substitute bread crumbs for the potatoes, add an extra egg and omit the milk.

Salads

TWELVE TO TWENTY-FOUR HOUR SALAD

1 large head lettuce
1 cup chopped green pepper
1 cup chopped celery
1 cup chopped red, Bermuda
   or spring onion
1 can drained peas (#303)

1 pint salad dressing or
   mayonnaise
2 teaspoon sugar
1 cup grated yellow cheese
1 bottle of bacon bits

Put layers of above items in this order. Spread salad dressing or mayonnaise over top. Sprinkle sugar over this and add cheese and bacon bits on top. Do not mix. Refrigerate 12-24 hours until ready to toss and serve. Makes 24 servings.

POTATOLESS POTATO SALAD

1 large head cauliflower (fresh)
1 medium green pepper diced
2 ribs fresh celery
2 tablespoons dehydrated flakes or
   green onions diced

4 to 6 average size dill
   pickles diced
Add powdered chicken or
   onion boullion

Cook cauliflower until it is done yet firm. Let cool. Add celery, pepper and pickles. Add seasoning, salt and pepper to taste. Mix with mustard to give consistency. Accent may be used. Mix well.

MOTHER'S 24 HOUR SALAD

1 tablespoon butter	1 egg
1 teaspoon mustard	1 pint whipping cream
1 tablespoon flour	1 can chunk pineapple
½ cup sugar	1 cup small marshmallows
1 cup boiling water	2 packages slivered almonds
½ cup vinegar	

Make paste of butter, mustard, flour and eggs. Add to boiling water and add sugar. Cook until thick, stirring constantly. Cool. Add 1 pint whipping cream and pour over pineapple, marshmallows and almonds. Refrigerate over night. Serve on lettuce leaf.

RASPBERRY DELIGHT SALAD

1 package raspberry gelatin	1 - 9 oz. canned crushed
1 cup hot water	pineapple
1 cup vanilla ice cream	½ cup chopped pecans
	1 medium banana

Combine gelatin with hot water. Add ice cream and stir until dissolved thoroughly. Combine undrained pineapple, nuts and sliced banana. Add to gelatin, pour into mold, chill until firm.

Meat and Poultry

CHICKEN CASSEROLE

1 package wild rice (cook	¼ cup chopped onion
as directed, drained)	Small jar pimentos
1 - 16 oz. French green beans	1 can water chestnuts (drained
1 can cream of celery soup	and sliced)
½ cup Miracle Whip	2 cups chopped, boiled chicken

Mix all ingredients together, put in greased baking dish and bake 20 minutes at 350 degrees. Then add topping and bake 15 minutes more.

TOPPING: Melt 4 tablespoons margarine and add ¾ (8 oz.) bag of Pepperidge Farm dressing mix.

PORK CHOP PIQUANT

4 large or 6 medium pork chops	1 can cream mushroom soup
1 egg slightly beaten	Worcestershire sauce
3 tablespoons water	Salt and pepper
1 cup bread crumbs	1 Bermuda onion, sliced

Dip each pork chop in a mixture of beaten egg and water; roll in bread crumbs. Brown chops lightly in small amount of fat in large frying pan. Top each chop with 1 tablespoon condensed mushroom soup to which ½ teaspoon Worcestershire sauce has been added. Sprinkle with salt and pepper. Add a slice of onion on top of each pork chop. Cover and simmer for about 45 minutes or until chops are tender.

PEPPER STEAK

1½ lb. round steak (cut in
  ½ inch strips)
¼ cup flour
½ teaspoon salt
⅛ teaspoon pepper
¼ cup oil or Crisco
1 cup tomatoes

1¾ cup water
½ cup chopped onions
Small clove garlic (minced or
  powdered) to taste
1 beef flavored bouillon cube
½ teaspoon Worcestershire sauce
2 large green peppers cut in strips

Cut steak into strips. Combine sale, flour and pepper. Coat meat strips and cook in hot oil until brown. Drain tomatoes. Add water, using liquid, onion, garlic and beef bouillon, and simmer. Cover meat and simmer until tender. Add pepper strips and simmer another 5 minutes. If necessary, add flour to make gravy mixture then add tomatoes and cook another 5 minutes. Serve over hot rice.

Bread and Cookies

SWISS TREATS

1 cup butter or oleo
1¼ cup sugar
1 egg, beaten
1 teaspoon vanilla
2½ cups sifted flour
1½ teaspoons baking powder

½ teaspoon salt
½ cup chopped pecans
½ cup maraschino cherries, cut up
½ cup flaked coconut
1 package 6 oz. chocolate chips

Cream butter, add sugar gradually. Blend in eggs and vanilla. Combine flour, baking powder and add salt. Add to creamed mixture. Blend well. Add nuts, cherries, coconut and chocolate chips. Mix well. Spread batter in greased 11x16 inch cookie sheet. Bake for 20 minutes in 375 degree oven. Cool slightly and cut into bars.

CEREAL - PEANUT BARS

½ cup light corn syrup
¼ cup brown sugar
Dash salt
1 cup crunchy peanut butter
1 tsp. vanilla

2 cups crisp rice cereal
1 cup corn flakes, slightly crushed
1 package 6 oz. semisweet
  chocolate chips

Combine syrup, sugar and salt in saucepan. Bring to a full boil. Stir in peanut butter. Remove from heat. Stir in vanilla, cereals and chocolate chips. Press into a buttered loaf pan. Chill one hour. Cut into small bars or squares.

COCOA BROWNIES

¾ cup all purpose flour
¾ cup granulated sugar
¼ teaspoon salt
¼ cup cocoa
½ cup oleo (softened), not melted

2 eggs
1 teaspoon vanilla
1/3 cup nuts (chopped)
1 tablespoon powdered sugar
   (if desired)

Sift flour, measure and resift with sugar, salt and cocoa. Add oleo, unbeaten eggs and vanilla. Beat on medium speed (or beat with wooden spoon 100 strokes per minute) for 3 minutes. Add nuts during last few seconds of beating. Turn into a greased pan, 7x11x½ inches and spread out in even layer. Bake in 350 degree oven for 15 to 18 minutes. Do not over bake. Let cool in pan then cut into squares. Sprinkle with powdered sugar if desired.

SEVEN LAYER COOKIES

¼ lb. butter or margarine
1 cup graham cracker crumbs
1 cup coconut (flaked)
1 6 oz. pkg. chocolate chips

1-6 oz. pkg. butterscotch chips
1 can sweetened condensed milk
1 cup chopped pecans

Melt butter in 9x13x2 inch cake pan. Cool slightly and grease sides of pan. Sprinkle graham cracker crumbs evenly over melted butter. Cover with flaked coconut. Follow with chips over coconut. Drizzle sweetened condensed milk over all. Sprinkle chopped pecans over top. Bake 30 minutes in preheated oven, 350 degrees. Cool and cut in squares.

PINEAPPLE DROP COOKIES

½ cup shortening
1 cup brown sugar
¾ cup crushed pineapple
¼ teaspoon salt
¼ teaspoon soda

¼ teaspoon baking powder
2 cups sifted flour
½ cup chopped nuts
1 teaspoon vanilla
1 egg

Cream together shortening and brown sugar. Add egg. Then add the pineapple, drained. Next sift all dry ingredients together and add to the first mixture. Add the chopped nuts and vanilla. Mix well. Drop by teaspoon on oiled baking sheet. Bake for 12 minutes in 425 degree oven.

ONE HOUR BUTTERMILK ROLLS

2 cakes yeast (dry)
¼ cup warm water
1½ cups buttermilk, luke warm
3 tablespoon sugar
½ cup melted shortening (or
   cooking oil is quicker)

1 egg, beaten
4½ cups flour
½ teaspoon soda
½ teaspoon baking powder
1 teaspoon salt

Crumble yeast into warm water. Add buttermilk, sugar and shortening. Add one egg, well beaten. Sift into this mixture the flour, soda, baking powder and salt. Beat smooth and let stand ten minutes. Roll out and shape into rolls. Let rise 30 minutes in warm place. Bake at 400 degrees about 15-20 minutes.

Cake and Pastry

RHUBARB COBBLER

1 lb. rhubarb	1½ teaspoon baking powder
1 cup sugar	½ teaspoon salt
½ teaspoon cinnamon	¼ cup lard or vegetable
1 cup flour	shortening
1 tablespoon sugar	1/3 cup milk

Set out 1½ quart baking dish. Wash and cut off leaves and stems from rhubarb. (Peel if tough). Cut into 1 inch lengths. Put into baking dish and toss gently with 1 cup sugar and ½ teaspoon cinnamon. Arrange rhubarb in even layers and dot with butter or margarine. Bake at 350 degrees for 20 minutes. Meanwhile: Sift together in a bowl, flour, 1 tablespoon sugar, baking powder and salt. Cut into dry ingredients lard or vegetable shortening. Make a "well" in center of the mixture and pour in all at one time 1/3 cup milk. Stir with fork until dough follows it. Remove rhubarb from oven and set control at 450 degrees. Drop tablespoon of dough over top of hot rhubarb. Return to oven and bake 10 minutes to 15 minutes longer. Serve warm with cream. Makes 6 servings.

NUTTY PEACH CRISP

1 can (29 oz.) sliced peaches (with syrup)	½ cup butter or margarine (melted)
1 pkg. butter pecan cake mix	1 cup flaked coconut
	1 cup chopped pecans

Heat oven to 325 degrees. Layer ingredients in order listed in ungreased oblong pan, 13x9x2 inches. Bake 55 to 60 minutes. Let stand at least 15 minutes before serving. Serve warm or cool and if desired, with sweetened whipped cream or ice cream. Serves 12 to 15.

FRUIT CAKE

1 cup butter	2 boxes raisins (white & dark each)
2 cups sugar	1 box currents
6 eggs	2 lbs. figs (ground in chopper)
3½ cups flour	2 boxes diced fruit (2 lbs.)
1 cup buttermilk	1 lb. red and green cherries
1 cup sweet milk	(½ lb. each)
2 teaspoon baking powder	1-10 oz. or 12 oz. pecans (2 cups)

Mix first 7 ingredients then add fruit in a large bowl. Pour batter over fruit mix and nuts and mix well. Pack in 10 inch tube pan, bake in over 300 degrees covered with foil for 3½ hours. Remove foil and bake ½ hour for browning. When cold, wrap in foil and store 1 month before using. Do not soak in anything. Cake will be naturally moist.

BANANA SPLIT CAKE

First Layer: Blend 2 cups graham crackers, 6 tablespoons melted margarine and ¼ cup sugar. Pack into pan.

Second Layer: Cream together ¾ stick margarine, 2 cups confectioners' sugar, add 2 eggs and 1 teaspoon vanilla. Pour over graham cracker mixture.

Third Layer: Slice 3 or 4 bananas over creamy filling.

Fourth Layer: Drain well, No. 2 can of crushed pineapple, spoon over bananas.

Fifth Layer: 1 pkg. Cool Whip, spread over pineapple.

Sixth Layer: Top with maraschino cherries.

Seventh Layer: Sprinkle chopped pecans over all.

Chill for one hour or more in refrigerator.

Candy

CHINESE NOODLE CANDY

2 packages butterscotch bits   1 bag Spanish peanuts
1 can Chinese noodles #2

Melt butterscotch bits on low heat, add noodles and peanuts. Drop on wax paper.

CANDY COOKIES

4 cups sugar   1 cup milk
6 tablespoons cocoa   1 cup peanut butter
1 teaspoon salt   6 cups quick oats
½ lb. butter (2 sticks)

Mix sugar, cocoa, salt, butter and milk. Boil one minute. Remove from heat. Add peanut butter and oats. Stir well. Drop on wax paper by spoonfuls. After they have set, cover and store in the refrigerator.

CHOCOLATE DROPS

3-4 sq. unsweetened chocolate   16 marshmallows (quartered)
1 cup milk   2½ cups graham cracker crumbs
¼ teaspoon salt   1 cup walnuts, whole or coarse
2 cups sugar   1 teaspoon butter
1 teaspoon vanilla

Cook milk with chocolate over low heat. Stir for smoothness. Add sugar and salt. Stir until mixture boils, taking care to wash sugar crystals from sides of pan. Cook to soft ball (224 to 230 F.). Remove from heat. Add butter, vanilla, don't stir. Cool to lukewarm. Stir in remaining ingredients. Drop by teaspoonfuls on wax paper and cool. Makes 18 big treats.

Casseroles

HOT CASSEROLE

1 lb. ground chuck
1 large grated onion (or diced)
1 can cream of chicken soup
1 can cream of mushroom soup
1 small can green chili peppers
   (chopped)
Dorito chips
Cheddar cheese

Cook ground chuck and onions until done but not browned. Mix together the chicken soup, mushroom soup, milk and green chili peppers. Combine above mixtures then alternate layers of Dorito chips and the mixture in a casserole dish. Top with grated Cheddar cheese and bake in a medium oven, 350 degrees, until thoroughly heated and bubbly.

GLORIFIED BROCCOLI

1 head of fresh broccoli or
   2 packages frozen broccoli
Cheddar cheese, sliced
1 can cream of mushroom soup
   or cream of chicken soup

Cook broccoli until tender. Drain. Put into greased casserole with sliced cheese placed into broccoli buds until well covered. Add soup and bake in oven 400 degrees until bubbly and cheese is melted. Can be started in Corning Ware. Makes 8 servings.

CASSEROLE DELUXE

2 cups sliced potatoes
1 cup sliced carrots
½ cup diced onions
½ cup diced celery
1 lb. ground beef
1 pint tomatoes
1½ teaspoons salt
½ teaspoon pepper

Layer all ingredients in greased baking dish. Cover and bake at 350 degrees for 30 minutes. Reduce temperature to 325 degrees. Bake, uncovered, until done. Yields 8 servings.

SPANAKOPETA (Broccoli or Spinach Squares)

¼ lb. melted butter
1 teaspoon baking powder
7 tablespoons flour
8 oz. shredded Brick cheese
16 oz. cottage cheese
1 package frozen broccoli
   or spinach
6 or 7 beaten eggs

Mix together and bake in a greased 13x8 inch baking dish at 350 degrees for 45 minutes to 1 hour.

THE PERFECT GIFT

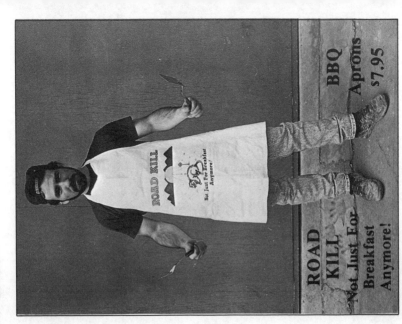

ROAD KILL
Not Just For Breakfast
Anymore!

BBQ
Aprons
$7.95

BOOK I

$7.95

BOOK II

$7.95

**GOURMET STYLE
ROAD KILL COOKING**
And Other Fine Recipes

**ROAD KILL COOKING
REDNECK STYLE**
And More Tails From The Fast Lane

*Hilarious Roadkill Recipes written in verse.
Real wild game and country recipes in back section of book.
Plastic Spiral Bound • Approximately 50 pgs.*

Road Kill
Brand
Pickled
POSSUM
Parts
$3.50

Not
For
Human
Consumption

Road Kill
Brand
Armadilla
Parts
$3.50

(Please Print)

Name _____

Street _____

City _____

State & Zip _____

Description	Quantity	Price
	Subtotal	
	Please add $2.00 S/H per order	
	Total	2.00

Fast Delivery